TURN UP OR TURN AROUND YOUR MARRIAGE:

7 ESSENTIALS

GARY SINCLAIR

Colossians 3:17

TO: My wife and best friend Jackie with whom I've learned, grown, loved and experienced intimacy for four decades.

ABOUT THE AUTHOR

Gary has been married to Jackie since 1976, has two grown children and six grandsons. He has been a teacher, speaker, counselor, pastor and mentor in both a Christian school and three different churches. He is a writer of two blogs and has been published in a number of national publications including *Leadership Journal, Guideposts* and *Worship Leader Online.*

He has undergraduate and graduate degrees from Taylor University, Wayne State University and Grace Theological Seminary and also attended Dallas Theological Seminary.

You can follow him and contact him about ministry opportunities at: *garysinclairconnect.com* plus read his *Safe At Home* family blog at: *http://safeathomeblog.blogspot.com.*

And he would love to hear from you at: *gary.sinclair71@gmail.com*

CONTENTS

INTRODUCTION

Think back to your wedding day for a minute, will you?

Your family and friends were there, everyone was smiling, your spouse looked wonderful and you promised your best friend that would you love and cherish them, build them up and care for them in sickness and in health, for richer, for poorer or something like that.

And you meant every word. So did I nearly four decades ago now.

But something happened along the way. The glow and specialness of that wedding day wore off. You had to begin to make marriage actually happen while the challenges of everyday life reared their head all around you.

Bills had to be paid and someone had to work. If and when children came along their needs began to drain you of time, money and energy. Emotional and physical challenges perhaps added their toll and it seems like you have little time to connect with each other the way you did at first.

In fact I would guess that today your marriage is in one of three stages:

You are *OK, but plateauing*. Things are not awful but they're not great. You feel like you're growing very little and just existing much of the time. Your friends would think you are a happy couple but you know that you're not in so many ways.

Sure, you still have vacations, go to activities together and serve at church, but your habits and daily responsibilities take priority over any close, meaningful communication.

Or *your marriage is a mess*. You fight all the time but there is rarely resolution. You're staying together largely because of the kids, trying to hide at least some of the angst between you from them. You've tried counseling on and off but can never stay at it.

You have normal problems, ones that others have, but with you they seem to add more fuel to your anger and disappointment with each other. You've talked about or at least considered divorce but somehow you make it to the next crisis without taking that final step. You honestly don't believe there is a good solution but you keep going at least for a while.

Or you're really doing well but know marriage takes hard work. You are always open to learning from others and how to improve what you already have. You have problems, too, but you generally figure out a way to work through them.

You still enjoy the glow of your love and the specialness of your relationship but want to make sure you don't lose that over time.

Well, whatever stage you're in, this book can help you.

Is it a magic wand? No. These are not seven easy steps to a new marriage. You can't just check them off on a weekend and expect everything to be better. You will, I hope, discover some practical, helpful ideas especially in the last chapter, but you will have to go deeper than just superficial change.

I am simply offering seven essentials that every great marriage requires to grow, last and deepen. Each will require some sacrifice and work. Any great skill or talent may be expressed and performed uniquely but there are usually some basics that everyone with that gift must acquire. These are some of those basics for your marriage.

When our kids were still at home my wife would remind us all that things like meals and clean laundry didn't just happen. Somebody (most of the time my wife) had to work hard to put a nutritious meal on the table or to see that our clothes were washed each week.

We need to work with the same commitment and determination at our marriages. So as you read this book, commit now to take time to talk through some or all of the questions at the end of each chapter before reading on.

One or more may stimulate you to get some counseling and go even further below the surface. If so, please go get that help. One book is hardly a substitute for long-term effort and greater expertise.

You will be challenged to examine your inner thoughts while changing certain aspects of your lifestyle, how you use your time and what you make priorities. But those changes will be worth it because the most important relationship in your life apart from the one you have with God will be better.

And for you parents you will be directly and indirectly impacting your children because they will have a healthier marriage model from which to learn. Remember your home will perhaps be the only Marriage 101 class they will ever have.

So let's get started. You and your spouse might consider reading each chapter together. Others will prefer going through a section separately and talking about it later or using the discussion questions as a guide.

However you do it, *take your time!* Stop and ponder each chapter before you continue.

WARNING TO GUYS: Just getting through the book is NOT the goal!

I am hoping and praying whether you are a man or woman you will allow the book to get through YOU. But that won't happen if you hurry and don't follow through. Be sure you read the chapters in order. There is a reason why I've laid them out the way I have. Even the practical ideas won't work if you don't grasp some of the early concepts.

So, jump into the first essential. It's the foundation for the rest of the book. Thanks for starting this journey with me. I'm praying that someday you will look back and see that your marriage was transformed and that many of the changes started today!

ESSENTIAL 1: RE-THINK YOUR IDENTITY

"I don't have to worry about identity theft because no one wants to be me."
– Jay London

It started the day we were born. Who we think we are began to be shaped by how we were touched, the words said to us and the accolades received or wished for passionately.

We started to learn that some people like us and some do not. Many were pleased with our personality, abilities and personal likes but others rejected us.

Many were blessed with affirming, supportive parents, teachers, bosses and friends but others found some or all of them to be a curse of sorts. They didn't give us the positive regard and encouragement we had hoped for and in ways actually hurt our esteem.

The affirmed became adults who saw themselves in a generally positive light while the cursed began to fear that no one would like them.

As a result, the more we were around those who did not accept us the more we began to believe that our identity, who we are at least in our minds, was flawed. And flawed was unacceptable. We were confident that flawed people are less than adequate people.

In fact, most of us derive our identity or at least aspects of it from varying forms of perceived weak areas in our lives. I've found it helpful with people to ask them to fill in one or more of these blanks regarding themselves.

So try it yourself and consider what you would put in each blank.

I'm not _____

smart, attractive, educated enough, etc.

I can't _____

have children, get a job, go to school, get pregnant, etc.

I experience _____

depression, grief, chronic pain, other loss, etc.

In the past I _____

was divorced, got pregnant before marriage, was arrested, got fired, etc.

People have told me I _____

would never amount to anything, was a loser, should never have been born, etc.

You could probably add your versions of these fill-in's but hopefully you get the idea. From these perceived flaws we begin to develop identity describers and perspectives that we ultimately bring to our marriage.

We can begin to think I am a loser, I'm inadequate, I must prove myself, I can't measure up or a hundred other things. And as a result we eventually inaugurate a quest in ourselves to remove, overcome or hide those blemishes and get people to believe that we are really OK.

Much of life is consumed with passionately demanding that others see us differently than the tainted identity we believe we have inherited.

And in our marriage who is the primary person we require believe we are OK? Of course it's our spouse.

The problem is that our identity is really a mistaken identity. It's not truly who we are. We simply believe it is. I'll talk later in this chapter about where our identity must reside but let's stay for now with the problem of our mistaken identity and marriage.

I am not terribly handy. I'm just not. But I grew up in an extended family where a lot of people were. They could build stuff, re-wire a room, even a whole house, make their own furniture and of course repair most anything from the plumbing to the car to the door that wouldn't latch.

Me? I didn't have a clue. I guess I could hope that it was because no one ever showed me how but I'm not sure that would have helped. I don't have much aptitude for that kind of thing though deep in my soul I do wish that I could do those handyman kinds of tasks.

But I do remember hearing two things as a kid. Some important people in my life reminded me that I wasn't very good at anything mechanical. And second, I began to believe that good husbands and real men DID have those abilities.

So when I got married, I took on the challenge to be super-husband, Mr. Fix-It and try to care for anything my wife might need done. If the car needed repairs I wanted to take care of it. If a faucet broke I knew that I should be able to get out my wrenches, diagnose the problem and have it working again in no time.

I mean, other guys that I knew did that. Why shouldn't I?

So, I would be working on a leaky faucet, using my only two wrenches to take things apart and get that leak stopped. The problem was that I didn't really know how to do it and usually didn't have the right tools. The faucet would still leak.

Or the car would still run terribly. I couldn't cut the piece of molding correctly to fit. I had a few minor victories here and there but the big-time failures went on and on.

And while I'm not above having used an expletive now and then, I'm not one to run off a string of swear words either. That's just not me thankfully. But when I could not accomplish my goal with the car, faucet or piece of wood, I would literally fly into my own private (mostly) rage and be cussing with the best of the boys downtown.

Why?

Because *my identity was on the line*. It was mistaken for sure. It really wasn't at stake but I thought it was. I believed my worth as a man, husband, friend, provider and caregiver was in jeopardy because of my mechanical incompetence, at least in my mind. That was all that mattered. I was angry that something as small as a pipe or saw could steal my value as a man from me.

So consider what experiences, words said and failures have contributed to your identity and impacted your relationship with your spouse. If you think you're not smart and have even been treated that way much of your life, what will your reaction be when your spouse questions your idea, choice or action?

Most likely you will get angry and try to defend yourself. You may cover up your hurt for a while, but inside you will be fuming.

"How can he/she treat me so meanly?" you bemoan. You begin to think your spouse is always criticizing you. Couples tell me all the time that they argue over the dumbest things but in almost every case I discover that they are really arguing over who the other person thinks they are! They don't want to appear stupid or wrong or as having any flaw.

So rather than communicate effectively (*see Essential Six*) they believe they must be right and not look incompetent. They must win the battle every time or look bad and be reminded of their inadequacy.

I would bet that some of your arguments with your spouse are for that very reason. *You believe you must win!* You must not look inferior. You wrongly assumed that your spouse must always make you feel affirmed, valued and important. And when they don't you go to war.

My battles were not quite so overt but intense nonetheless. My war was mostly with myself knowing that I could not fix the faucet or the car or whatever. So I would simply make excuses as to why I couldn't get to that task. Yes, at times I would get irritated with my wife for even bringing up the problem suggesting that we could live with it and wondering out loud, "Why is this such a big deal?"

But the reasons were the same. I didn't want to be exposed in front of her as incompetent. In fact, later I realized that my struggle was really about just that – *competence*. I wrestled for years trying to find all sorts of ways to look good and have people like me. I still have twinges in my competence nerve (*there really is no such thing*) today but thankfully with God's help I've made some progress.

What identity issues have you dragged to your marriage? You have likely hung on to something hurtful from your past too and it's possible it is hamstringing your relationship and communication. Before you read on I suggest you think about how you would fill in the blanks on the earlier page.

It's important to admit that how you see yourself may be out of whack.

And if your identity is misaligned then you'll never do any of the practical things I suggest in *Essential Six* on communication. The tasks will simply be too scary and you will revert back to old habits and strategies. In addition you will never grow as a person, parent, Christian or friend.

Your mistaken identity will always hold you back. Maybe it's time to figure out or at least reconsider where your true identity, worth and value comes from.

THE SOURCE OF OUR REAL IDENTITY

First of all, let me suggest where our identity does NOT come from. Too many well-intended writers, educators and even doctors like to suggest that our self-esteem comes from human interaction, skill development, accomplishments and activities.

For example, they suggest that the words of parents or teachers, the successes in sports, music or classes and the like will build up a child's esteem. And I would suggest that those things can make a child feel better about himself or herself . . . but only for a while.

The problem is that if esteem and value are found in words and successful accomplishments then what happens to our worth when those words or achievements fade away due to age, declining skill level or rejection?

We can certainly improve or affirm worth through these human interactions and experiences but we can never assure it. Our identity must come from outside human experience and I am confident it only resides with God Himself. He is the one who made us, who provided a way of salvation and forgiveness in Jesus and who is the source of all love.

It makes sense that Someone who is beyond humanity is the only reliable source for keeping our worth and value intact.

In fact, there are five truths that every person who is a child of God, a follower of Christ can know and embrace every day no matter what else is going on in their life. No weakness, tendency, life circumstance or disappointment can ever take these five things away. Let me review them briefly.

You are loved. Is there anything else that humans crave more today than being loved? I don't think so. We long to be loved not for what we've done but who we are. We long for what Fred Rogers coined on his children's television show as being loved *just the way you are.*

And the Bible is filled with reminders of God's incredible, unconditional love for us. Perhaps the most familiar verse in the New Testament is John 3:16, *"For God so loved the world that He gave His only begotten son."*

Or Romans chapter 8 provides a long list of powers, beings and situations that can never separate us from the love of God. God's love is unbreakable and unshakable.

We must remember that our spouse, though likely wonderful in so many ways, can never love us enough. I have premarital couples all the time talk about their unconditional love for each other and I have to gently remind them that *no human can love unconditionally.* We can and should try but we won't do it.

Only God can. And He does. Our esteem must rest on that truth.

You matter. It's easy to also accept this idea that we really aren't that important to anyone and that no one notices us including God. We think He's probably too busy anyway to pay much attention to our life in general much less our struggles.

And yet He sent His son to literally die for us. That should tell us a lot about whether we matter to Him or not. We matter so much that He would do anything to make a way for us to be in His family.

We should perhaps think more like an adopted child (if you're adopted you have an advantage here) pondering the fact that some couple chose them out of thousands to be a part of their family. That child mattered to them so much that they loved them and invited them into their home for the rest of their lives.

Psalm 18:19 says it well from God's perspective as David wrote these words, *"He brought me out into a spacious place; he rescued me because He delighted in me." (NIV)*

That's the kind of mattering we can enjoy in God and need reminding of regularly.

Thirdly and closely related to mattering is this: **You have a purpose.**

Many people come to believe that they really aren't on this earth for any special reason other than to exist. They've never been told and considered the fact that God has a unique and special plan for them.

The good news is that every person has a purpose. You and I have unique circumstances to change, people to impact and goals to accomplish. You don't just have a family, job or circumstance. *You have a CALLING.*

Psalm 57:2, "I cry out to God Most High, to God, who fulfills his purpose for me." (NIV)

Again, growing up we may have felt unimportant, not as good or talented as others, berated and left behind. We may have seen others have more success, make more money and not face the personal challenges we did. And we may assume then that God has pretty much given up on us and put us out to pasture.

Wrong.

You still have purpose even if you've lost your job, can't finish school, are struggling with your kids, messed up big time or don't agree with your spouse.

Fourthly, **you are forgiven**. Have you brought some big-time mistakes to your marriage? Have you spent a lot of time and energy trying to cover them up, prop yourself up, hide from them or dull the pain that come from them?

Yes, there are often consequences whose effects may impact us the rest of our lives. But the sins are forgiven.

It's time to let them go. Perhaps you need to go back to your day of salvation and remember that Jesus really did die for ALL your sins, not just a few. He really did give us grace. Your identity is no longer wrapped up in the wrong you committed. God sees them no more. You don't have to fight for your worth on this spectrum either.

And if you've never trusted in Jesus, then how about now? You can discover a new identity, join God's family, know you're forgiven and have life for eternity with God. You'll get power to live differently and begin to change from the inside out. (See a sample prayer that I put at the end of this chapter.)

And fifthly, *you are a child of God.* When we invite Christ in and ask for God's forgiveness, we become a child of God, an adopted member of His family. And like it is with human families, children can't be un-born.

Sure the relationship can be tarnished, stressed and distant, but a child is always the child of his or her parents. The same is true of our relationship with God. Our loving parent will always cherish us, welcome us back and long for our good.

If you're familiar with the prodigal son story in Luke 15, you know that a young son, one of two, asked for his inheritance early and left home. He eventually squandered everything and realized that he needed to go back.

However, as the parable goes, the father actually saw the son coming the day he returned. *"But while he was still a long way off, his father saw him and was filled with compassion for him."* (v. 20) How did his father see him if the boy had been gone for months maybe years as implied in the parable?

The father had to be looking for him every day!

And our Father will always be looking for us even when we stray. We're one of His, He loves us, we matter, we still have purpose and we're forgiven. That's where our true *identity* is found!

If you want to start changing your marriage (and your life in general) then you need to make sure that your identity has the proper foundation and source. You may have lived your whole life thinking that your marriage must change who you are.

You have lived defending, arguing and demanding that people see you differently when God has seen you all along as His child who He unconditionally loves.

It's time to walk into the rest of your life as a truly new person, one who doesn't have to derive his or her value from somewhere else, including your spouse.

You will be freer to enter in to challenges, to make appropriate changes and even deal with conflict when your personhood isn't on the line. In fact, you will begin to relate better at work, church, with other relatives and in your community by knowing who you really are.

Take your case of mistaken identity today to God and thank Him for making you who He made you to be. Walk through some of the questions at the end of the chapter, too, before you move on and put a new stake in the ground regarding your more accurate view of you.

Pray the prayer below if you've never done that before. Go find a pastor, friend or other leader who can tell you what next steps to take to grow in your new faith.

You're never going to be the same!

A prayer of salvation: "Dear God, thank you for loving me and giving me an opportunity to join your family. Thank you for sending Jesus to die in my place, take my sin and selfishness on Himself, then rise again overcoming death and making a way for me to get to You. Today I receive your gift of eternal life and invite Jesus into my heart and life. Begin to change me from the inside out and help me grow in my new faith. Today I know that I'm your child. Amen.

Today's date – I prayed this prayer for the first time and received Jesus.

DIGGING DEEPER INTO ESSENTIAL 1

1. Fill in any more of the blanks that I left you to consider concerning your identity. You might even ask your spouse for their thoughts and see if they agree.

2. Write down how that false identity has impacted you in your life in general. What are some of the general tendencies you have in your relationships in general?

3. Ponder and discuss with your spouse ways that each other's mistaken identity has impacted your marriage – i.e. communication, ways of relating, emotions, etc.

4. Study the scripture references in this chapter committing any that are particularly impacting for you to memory.

5. Write down the list of five things I suggested are always true of any Christ follower. Start taking them with you and reminding yourself of them everyday.

ESSENTIAL 2: UNDERSTAND REAL INTIMACY

*"I am certain that most couples expect to find intimacy in marriage, but somehow it eludes them." – **James Dobson***

When you observe or hear the word intimacy in a magazine article title, television teaser or movie trailer, what do you pretty much assume the topic will be?

Yep. Sex.

And sex is a good thing in the right setting. God invented it. He expects and encourages us to enjoy it in the context of marriage and even gave us in the Bible one of the sexiest books ever written, *The Song of Solomon.*

There's nothing wrong with sex or the pleasure it gives. It is through that wonderful experience of *lovemaking* that children are born. What better way to bring our little ones into this world than through an act of love.

But *sex isn't all there is to intimacy*. The media and entertainment worlds have not helped us here by suggesting that it is. And they sadly often turn physical oneness into a joke or mere hobby much of the time.

Nonetheless, let's carefully use the act of sex to help us discover what total intimacy might look like. Physical sex involves *a mutually desired disrobing or exposure of one another for the purpose of passionately expressing love through extreme closeness and one-ness.*

In fact, God told us in the very first book of the Bible that this kind of intimacy is foundational to every marriage. "For this reason a man will leave his father and mother and be united to his wife, and they will become one flesh." Genesis 2:24

One flesh.

But that oneness or one flesh was to go far beyond the physical realm. Oneness involves the whole person and to focus only on the sexual act misses *going all the way* as the old colloquialism for sex used to suggest.

So what else does intimacy involve?

Let's again look to the Bible for guidance. The book of I Thessalonians wraps up with the inclusion of these words. *"May your whole spirit, soul and body be kept blameless at the coming of our Lord Jesus Christ."*

We're apparently made of three dimensions: *spirit, soul and body.* Some have argued, rightly so, that spirit and soul have a unique connection, even overlapping dimension. However, since scripture uses soul and spirit distinctively and because there are helpful lessons and implications that result, let's stay with all three.

Body, soul and spirit make up a trilogy of components where in marriage we can enjoy and develop true intimacy.

In fact, these three dimensions actually function concurrently. As we grow in spirit and soul, our physical intimacy grows. As we enhance our spiritual and physical intimacy we will become more emotionally intimate.

Interestingly many couples find that after a few years of marriage, their sex life has become boring, bland and even more sporadic. They don't dislike it or each other but there's not the spark that there used to be. In many cases their problem is not physical but is the result of a lack of spirit and soul intimacy.

SO WHAT ARE SPIRIT AND SOUL INTIMACY ANYWAY?

Spirit intimacy is what we enjoy when our relationship with God through our own spirit connects with the other person. There is certainly no special formula here but some of our spiritual connections will come through the obvious and regular disciplines of mutual *prayer, worship and Bible study.*

Even when we simply discuss our personal experiences or responses in those activities we can meaningfully engage in spiritual intimacy. Perhaps you talk about the message you heard in church on the weekend or the Bible passage you recently read or studied in a group you attend. Maybe you share how a new worship song is particularly meaningful to you.

Any of those interactions will help you find spiritual intimacy.

But notice that not all spiritual connecting has to be done together. The reality is that as each of you gets closer to God, you will naturally get closer to each other.

Consider the triangle below.

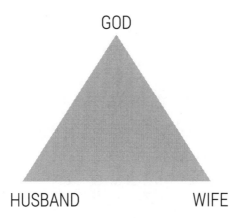

Put a dot in your mind somewhere on the side between husband and God. Then put another dot, not necessarily at the same level, between God and the wife. Let each of those dots represent where both spouses' relationships with God are at present.

Now draw a line between the two dots. Notice that this line is shorter than the distance the husband and wife were at the bottom.

When each partner works at their relationship with God they naturally get nearer to one another and more intimate!

And as you each grow spiritually and then begin to connect more and more in the areas of prayer, worship and Bible study you will gravitate to other spiritual growth activities and commitments.

OTHER SPIRITUAL GROWTH IDEAS FOR A COUPLE.

Serve together. Work together in a ministry at your church, take a missions trip, volunteer in a community non-profit or come up with your own ministry to others.

My wife Jackie and I during the last twenty years have developed a heart for Russia allowing me to have traveled there so far some sixteen times. But she has gone on three of those trips and we have had scores of Russian friends in our home.

This is not my ministry. It has become our ministry.

Over the years we have also helped in nurseries, led college and singles ministries, sung in music groups and served in other church serving opportunities both separately and together and our spiritual intimacy has grown as a result.

Teach your children. They always say the teacher learns more than the student and that is certainly true when you try to instruct your kids in their spiritual growth. Work together with your spouse to figure out how to make your faith come alive at home.

There are thousands of ideas on the Internet and many churches actually provide companion materials for parents that mirror what the children are learning at church. Use them. Pray with one another as a family. Make your faith a natural thing at home.

As you do, you and your spouse will find yourselves more and more on the same page with God as you train up your children in the way they should go. (Proverbs 22:6)

SO WHAT IS SOUL INTIMACY?

Soul intimacy is the connection you and your spouse have emotionally. It is the exposing and connecting of your feelings, thoughts, goals and dreams. It's who you really are apart from the skin!

But this is a scary place for many, if not most, couples to go. It's threatening because going here may require hearing some things that you don't want to hear such as that you were wrong or made a mistake or hurt the other person in some way.

It initiates fear because you won't always know what to say or do when one or both of you goes beneath the surface to reveal what you're really thinking or feeling.

And if your *identity* is mistaken you will think when you hear those words that your worth is on the line and rather than move toward your spouse will fight or flee.

Or you may feel inadequate to understand the other person so you simply avoid going deep with them. Guys tend to do this more than women and often use busyness, humor, hobbies, being tough and a host of other things to avoid the emotional world of their wives.

Women on the other hand once they sense an opening can say too much, never quit talking and as Robert Gottman suggests *flood* their husband with more emotional information than he can handle at one time. Nonetheless, emotional intimacy is crucial to a healthy marriage and spouses must be willing to work at learning to engage in it well.

And while emotional intimacy is fueled and sweetened by healthy communication, something I will develop in *Essential 6*, let me provide some important foundational thoughts here.

LAYING THE GROUNDWORK FOR SOUL INTIMACY

Abilities like a great golf swing, cooking or an apprenticed skill may vary but there are certain basics to each talent that are the underpinnings for all who succeed.

Jordan Speith, for example, hits the ball differently than Phil Mickelson but there are still some fundamentals that both would agree are essential to world class golf.

The same is true for connecting emotionally. We will all have unique personalities, backgrounds and circumstances but there are some basics everyone needs to know and utilize in some way to connect well.

Let me suggest a few.

We must learn to listen. As one of my mentors, Larry Crabb, used to say we must learn to listen *beneath the words*. I'll help you more with that in a later chapter. Nonetheless, growing couples practice listening well.

They turn off the television, avoid distractions and don't allow themselves to always dominate the conversation.

We must make time for each other. I'll speak about this one in several contexts including *Essential 3* but great communication and connection will never occur if we have no time or are rushed. Today's families are run by the tyranny of the urgent or at least the tyranny of our children's sports and other activities schedules.

So many couples are driven by myriad activities in their lives thinking they are providing one another all the wonderful experiences they must have when in reality they are potentially stealing intimacy from one another.

For our entire marriage Jackie and I have pretty much carved out a time each week that was just for us whether we had kids or not. Sometimes it was only a half day, other times a full one. We made deals with other couples to watch each other's children so we wouldn't have to spend extra money for babysitting when funds were tight. It can be done but you have to work at it.

We must avoid soul killers. The book of Proverbs contains a very sobering phrase about communication. In chapter 18, verse 21, it says, *"The tongue has the power of life and death..."* Wow, we can kill someone with our words?

Well, not typically, though bullying these days has had some pretty tragic results especially among young people. However, I think this verse refers most often to the idea that our words can *kill,* so to speak, someone's personhood. We leave huge scars and potential wounds when we attack the soul.

How? With *words of death*... words that attack the character, name-calling, comparisons to others, saying *you always* and *you never*. When we are always defensive, critical, silent or shaming one another we can attack the other in the deep recesses of the heart and communication is for the most part impossible. More on this in *Essential 6* as well.

We must learn and respond to our spouse's love languages. Many have read the wonderful book by Gary Chapman that explains how each of us has certain love languages, ways that love is expressed to them, that really resonates with them.

We need to figure out what language(s) our spouse speaks and dish out large helpings of that kind of love to them. And if we're not very good at that language ourselves (which is typical) then we need to practice that language even more.

Chapman suggests the five languages are:

- **Gifts**: Cards, roses, candy, special surprises, etc.
- **Acts of Service**: The things we do every day to help out one another.
- **Affirmation:** Words that build up and go deeply into the soul
- **Physical touch:** Touch that doesn't necessarily lead to more.
- **Focused time:** Time that is just for the other person without distractions.

Let me suggest a fun exercise. Have each of you write down what you think are your *top two gifts that you often give to the other per-*

son. These come naturally and easily for you and you hardly have to think about them

Second, each write down the top two *gifts that make you feel loved* by the other, ones you either already get or would like more of. Work on your lists separately and then share them with each other.

There are no right answers but my hunch is that you will find that the gift you would like to most receive is *not* the first or second gift of the other person.

Whatever the result you'll learn some ways to better love your spouse and to enjoy greater soul intimacy.

We need some practical help, ideas and structure. We must actually practice and learn to communicate effectively, exploring one another's emotions and walking deeply into the heart of the other. In fact I've written a whole chapter on that and will discuss this concept in more detail in *Essential 6*.

You see intimacy is a lot more than a physical union of two people. It's also a *spirit and soul union*. But sadly most couples are taught little about spirit and soul connection so they simply avoid it much of the time and their marriage suffers as a result.

Start now to work on these fundamentals in your relationship. They will set the stage for greater communication which I will talk about near the end of the book.

KEEPING ROMANCE (BODY INTIMACY) ALIVE.

And before we end this chapter let's not forget the *physical part.* Of course if you work on soul and spirit you will automatically help your physical intimacy. Remember the three parts work together in many ways.

However, it's important to also give your body intimacy some special attention. Here are a few ideas:

Set time and resources aside to get away now and then. Often just getting out of the house and doing something different can spice up your romance. You don't have to spend lots of money. You might choose a nice hotel nearby or tack your time on to the end of a conference that one of you must attend.

Plan some romantic dates. There are lots of great little books out there that contain romantic date ideas which can be fun. You will have to make time for these but sharing the responsibility for the planning or working on them together can help you overcome the time crunch.

Be intentional about touching. When is the last time you held hands, went to a movie and snuggled, watched television with the lights low or kissed each other for longer than one second? Having children, being busy or getting tired can steal much of our time, energy and available hands that we would normally give to touch so being purposeful is essential.

We used to joke that during our early parenting years we forgot how to hold hands because one hand was always connected to one of the kids. It wasn't totally a joke but thankfully we worked at touching anyway.

Read a book or article on marriage and sexuality. Cliff and Joyce Penner have, in my opinion, some of the best materials out there from a Christian and practical perspective. Commit to reading one of their books or something similar this year. I've put a few ideas at the end of the chapter.

Avoid improper and unguarded intimacy with someone else of the opposite sex. Because intimacy is such a powerful commodity it can develop in another relationship under the right (or wrong, I guess) conditions.

The relationship starts simply enough. We end up in close proximity to someone at work, in the neighborhood, at the gym or as part of a church group. Conversations are at first casual but the other person starts to tell us how valuable we are, how much we've helped them, how attractive we are on a given day or how much they are struggling at home with their spouse (*soul intimacy*).

As a result we work out together more, have coffee or lunch or just see each other a little more often. And perhaps there's a lack of soul intimacy at home of late. Nothing major but we'd love more. And the attention from that other person starts to taste like water in the desert.

And if we're Christians we may even start to pray for each other, share Bible verses or other words of encouragement (*spirit intimacy*). We might even serve together at church and feel a sense of accomplishment and inspiration as we do the same project.

Pretty soon we're more eager to see that other person than we are our spouse. Why? Because we've shared a closeness, an intimacy of soul and spirit that we've been missing at home.

Guess what the only part of intimacy missing is? Of course, it's the physical. And that may start with just a hug or touch, but the pull now will be difficult to resist. That's often how affairs start.

GUARD YOUR HEART

Keep your heart with all dilligence, for out of it
spring the issues of life.
Proverbs 4:23

We must guard our heart from inappropriate intimacy with another person of the opposite sex who is not our spouse. *Stop it before it starts.* Let someone else be the confidante of that other person, not you. Enjoy the compliments you get, but don't go back for more.

I personally do not *ever* have a meal or coffee alone with a woman who is not my wife, mom, sister and daughter. Because I don't trust the woman? Nope. I don't trust me.

I know that I'm capable of being wooed by an attractive woman who thinks I'm wonderful or whom I'm serving with at church.

I know that I can be drawn in when someone values me and that it's even more alluring when that person is a gorgeous female half my age. I just can't go there and neither should you.

So it's possible that you and your spouse have never really understood the whole picture of marital intimacy. And that could be why your marriage is boring, struggling or simply not working.

Are you willing to try to find out before you give up?

I hope so. Take some of the concepts in this chapter and talk about them. Do the follow-up questions at the end of the chapter and dig a little deeper into what intimacy really means and could become for you and your spouse.

It's possible that the two of you will become closer than you've ever been and finally realized what you've been missing!

OTHER BOOK RECOMMENDATIONS:

Love and Respect, Emerson Eggerichs

Sacred Marriage, Gary Thomas

Marriage Builder, Larry Crabb

DIGGING DEEPER INTO ESSENTIAL 2:

1. Do the love languages exercise I gave you. Don't rush it.

2. Discuss which element of intimacy you think has been lacking most in your relationship and why. (Body, soul, spirit)

3. What steps will you both take to add more overall intimacy to your marriage?

4. Ask yourself if there are any relationships that you have with someone of the opposite sex that might be inappropriate or dangerous. If so, what do you need to do to change things?

5. Buy one of my book suggestions and read it together.

ESSENTIAL 3: ADD MARGIN TO YOUR LIFE

"Teach us to use wisely all the time that we have."
– Psalm 90:12 (CEV)

If you've ever written a comment on someone's blog or website you know that sometimes you get a message like, *"This comment awaiting moderation."* That means that someone needs to review your ideas, make sure they're not out of line, laced with profanity or too long.

Your words literally have to be reviewed by a moderator. It's a good idea unless they don't care what shows up on a public blog.

However, I wonder if that phrase shouldn't be written in bold letters somewhere for us spouses to see every day. *Awaiting moderation.* As we look at and think about our schedule, as we anticipate more requests and demands on our time, as the urgent needs of each other and our children beckon to us, maybe we need to stop and *think about some moderation first.*

How many marriages are slowly having the life sucked out of them because the husband and wife (and/or mom and dad) are simply too busy and need to slow down. They have no margin, especially to find room for strengthening their marriage relationship. Is that you and your spouse?

Awaiting moderation decisions might include: *general activities, kids' responsibilities, house maintenance projects, weekly chores, meetings outside the home, hobbies, educational demands, school service commitments, church obligations.* The list could go on and on, right? You can add your own that I didn't mention.

Remember in the last essential we said that focused time is a love language. We can't rush it. We dare not suggest that our short amount of time is quality time so that substitutes for quantity. That doesn't usually work.

Leaving space for the important things is called *adding margin*. Having margin in our lives is a choice, a lifestyle, a perspective, not a one-time event. It's not a take-a-weekend-off twice a year thing. It's not an *OK-I'll-turn-the-TV-off* for a few minutes deal.

"Okay, honey, I'll turn the TV off during half-time."

No, *margin is a very intentional commitment in a marriage by a husband and wife to be more in control of their time than their time is in control of them!* Having margin does not mean that we won't be busy. Rather it means that we know when to stop and avoid getting busier because it's not healthy or productive.

It may even be nearing destructive!

You see margin assures that we have time for each other in our marriage. As we'll see again in *Essential 6,* healthy soul connecting requires effective communication which requires a significant and regular block of time.

Soul connecting requires time to simmer, ponder, reflect and re-spond.

SO HOW DO WE GET MORE MARGIN?

First, *we need to do some spring cleaning of our schedule*. Like those items in our attic or closet we need to throw some activities and commitments away that were once meaningful to us but that we do not need anymore.

I know this can be emotionally difficult but here are a few questions that might prompt you to put something in your personal wastebasket or dumpster:

Do I dread this commitment more and more every time it comes around?

Do I fudge on my preparation and planning for it because I simply do not have time?

Do I see joy in others in my home when we're involved in it or could they just take it or leave it?

Are several of these activities just more of the same? Would I just rather be doing something else?

Was I (or we) doing this for all the wrong reasons?

Do I still feel an obvious calling from God or is this commitment just an obligation now?

When you've made your decisions on what to throw out *do it now*. Call the people you need to call, write the email that needs to be written or simply take it off your calendar. You may grieve it for a time and that's normal but don't look back.

In addition, talk about what things are we *missing out on, skimming on, barely doing but need to be doing* because other things are crowding them out? My hunch is that most parents had certain desires and goals for their families that have gotten lost because they're simply doing too much that doesn't really matter that much.

So start somewhere. Where can you trim? Where *must* you cut back? Then add one thing in that you'd rather be doing or need to do as a family that you'll all be glad you did later. And don't forget to include just some quiet time, time that doesn't have to be so productive and results oriented.

Second, *immediately pencil in some time for you and your spouse*. How you spend this time will probably evolve but for now start somewhere. Plan to go out each time or get a babysitter if needed and stay home. (NOTE: *Don't turn your new margin into more busyness.*)

But be intentional and start a new *habit* that includes some very intentional slowing down and just being together. Treat that time as somewhat sacred like Jackie and I did with our weekly schedule.

That way even if you have to miss your time one week it's been normalized enough that you automatically plan on it for the next week.

Third, *if you are a parent you will need to have your children cut back on some of their activities.* I realize that some of you who just read that statement are about to put the book down now but stay with me.

Our children cannot and should not become the center of our personal universe!

It's not healthy for them or our marriage. We will never have margin or time for re-fueling our marriage and our soul relationship if all we do is drive the taxi for our kids' multitude of activities. Talk with your children about what you're going to cut and why. Use this as a teaching and learning opportunity that they can take into their marriage someday.

They, too, need some margin and to learn to slow down, pace themselves and just enjoy being a child. Allow the new margin that you all enjoy to get you playing a few more games, watching a movie now and then and talking about life, dreams, hopes and who knows what else.

Take some time to re-think your family goals, purpose and direction. Most families plan for vacations, retirement, school and holidays but spend no time thinking about the direction of their family and why they are headed that way.

If we were to seriously consider the major goals we have, the ones that *really* matter, the things we long to have accomplished in ten or twenty years, we would change our lifestyles in a heartbeat.

So take inventory, have a couple's leadership meeting and get focused again. You'll probably find other things that can go that won't matter that much.

Develop more financial margin. Much of our stress and time crunch these days can be attributed to our challenges with money. And for some of us there's not much we can do. We're working hard, trying to trim expenses and still barely getting by.

However, it's possible that some of your lack of margin is your own fault. Things can be improved by downsizing, cutting back and/ or getting out of debt. Many others such as Dave Ramsey have written entire books on financial planning and management so if you need help seek out their books, seminars or others who are experts in finance.

Nonetheless, think about the freedom that comes when with a budget you actually have money in an account and can spend it without pressure or guilt. The same can be true with your time, including time with your spouse.

Finally, *don't add new things. Only substitute and drop.* As I write I am paring down my book collection. But thankfully, a number of years ago I decided on a new plan.

Every time I buy or receive a new book I get rid of one. I either throw it away or give it to someone or an organization who can use it. That has kept my already large library from growing even more. I want more margin when it comes to space.

Too many activities and not enough margin adds emotional weight to our lives and relationships that can be harmful. We would be wise to cut some of the extra weight out of our world by adding more time.

SOME ADDITIONAL BENEFITS OF MARGIN

Of course margin will help your marriage but there are some other benefits worth noting, most of which will indirectly help your spousal intimacy too:

Less stress. You will worry about less, be less tense about traffic and being late. You will eat meals together a little more often and not find yourself running into the house for a few minutes only to have to leave again. You might find yourself reading that novel you've wanted to dig into or that inspirational book that seemed so compelling.

More energy. You will have more interest in time with your spouse of course but you will be more eager to spend time with the other important people in your life or to exercise at your own pace or to enjoy an activity that is just for you.

More time for God. Of course God is with us wherever we go, but lack of margin tends to steal our extended devotional time first. With some new time in our schedule we can slow down as we read the Bible, pray or meditate. We can feel freer to get up a little earlier, take a prayer retreat now and then or just meditate on the day.

Greater reserves for emergencies. Just like when we have savings set aside for a new stove or refrigerator when it breaks, margin is our savings account for life's unexpected challenges. We not only have more time but we have more emotional and spiritual reserves with which to take on the newest struggle.

New perspective. After living with more margin for a while, you will also start to wonder how you lived for so long under the pressure you lived under. You will start to look at your goals and priorities differently and be okay with accomplishing less better.

You will likely during this time get more focused or perhaps honed in for the first time on a calling from God rather than just a job or a bunch of extra activities. You will find you and your spouse are getting to taste intimacy of body, soul and spirit at a whole new level.

My hunch is that others will also see the difference and wonder what has made the change. Tell them. Tell them how your life was turned around when you slowed down. Maybe they will do the same.

DIGGING DEEPER INTO ESSENTIAL 3

1. Talk with each other about the components of your life that are stealing margin from you the most?

2. Make a list of where you could cut things and begin to add some needed margin to your life.

3. If you had more margin, what kind of activity could you add that would give you more time together and be something you both enjoy?

4. Put one instance of that activity on your calendar.

ESSENTIAL 4: BECOME FRIENDS AGAIN

It is not a lack of love, but a lack of friendship that makes unhappy marriages.
– **Friedrich Nietzsche**

Ryan and Allison are on their fourth date. They've moved beyond the awkwardness of two people who just met to truly looking forward to being with each other.

Earlier tonight they sat at one of their favorite restaurants for over two hours just talking, enjoying good food and drink, laughing at each other's silly comments and detailing some of their favorite trips, bands and movies.

Scores of other people came in and out of the dining area but they hardly noticed them. Finally at one point they spontaneously decided to just walk hand-in-hand through the well-lit and safe downtown area. This time there were hundreds of others doing the same but that mattered little to them.

They had no agenda but their fun conversation continued from right where it left off at dinner. At times they just admired the city's beauty, bright lights and the fresh, cool air that they'd missed during the week when at work.

Soon a coffee shop came into view and they decided to take another thirty minutes and enjoy their favorite lattes along with some more conversation at a little table that overlooked the street.

The couple found themselves starting to talk a bit more deeply at that point. They started to explore their dreams, hopes of new job opportunities, other places to visit someday, personal goals to reach and spiritual commitment possibilities.

Neither cared too much whether those hopes were realistic. It was just fun to hear the other person get excited about the future. Perhaps they would enjoy some of those things together.

I would guess that many of us remember similar times with our spouse or a former partner. We were less stressed, more spontaneous and eager to spend time with this special person.

We relished being friends and the benefits that come with a healthy and warm relationship. Friendship wasn't a luxury then. It was normal. Time was less structured and we couldn't wait for the next time.

You see there are things that good friends just do, even when they are married. In fact, let me suggest a list of words that most friends would agree are pretty typical at some point within their relationship.

Check out my list. Then ask yourself how many of those words are commonplace when the two of you are together. If there are at least 8-10 that you can include you may be doing pretty well on friendship. But if there are only a couple on your list, you probably have some significant work to do in growing this vital component of a great marriage.

THINGS FRIENDS DO OR EXPERIENCE

Spontaneity	List-making	Engagement
Fun	Teasing	Planning
Laughter	Talking	Anticipation
Dreaming	Feeling relaxed	Listening

However, many of us are probably saying, *But now we're married. Life has gotten more complicated. We just don't have time for all this.*

Perhaps we've started our family. Our job is overwhelming and we have so many responsibilities now. And while we may be married, lovers, housemates, parents and leaders, too few of us are still doing much to act like friends. People suggest in social media all the time that they are still in love with their best friend, but do they act like it?

We look may look at my fictitious couple, Ryan and Allison, and think, "Nope, that will never be us again. We can't afford to make time to do that anymore."

Well, let me tell you why you can't afford NOT to make the time. It may surprise you, but the leading cause of troubled marriages is not lack of communication, poor sex, financial strain or lousy in-laws. Yes, those things are important. *However, the number one marriage wrecker is when couples lose their ability or commitment to be friends.*

That's not me suggesting that. It's documented by one of the top marriage experts in the country, Dr. John Gottman, among others.

He suggests that *happy marriages place an emphasis on developing, growing and maintaining their friendship. They invest in one another emotionally. They listen to the others fears, hopes, dreams, and aspirations. They take mental notes of what the other person likes and dislikes.*

They think about the other person in a positive light and overlook their shortcomings. In other words, they make the other person a priority. They keep things personal. They don't invest in an idea. They invest in a person.

That's what friends do!

One place to start is to get to simply get to know your spouse better. How well do you really know each other? Probably not as well as you may think.

To find out, try taking the following quiz, adapted from one of Gottman's books. Answer each question True or False.

- I can name my partner's best friends.
- I know what stresses my partner currently faces.
- I know the names of those who have been irritating my partner lately.
- I know some of my partner's life dreams.
- I am very familiar with my partner's religious beliefs.
- I can outline my partner's basic philosophy of life.

- I can list the relatives my partner likes least.
- I know my partner's favorite music.
- I can list my partner's favorite three movies.
- I know the most stressful thing that happened to my partner in childhood.
- I can list my partner's major aspirations.
- I know what my partner would do if he/she won a million dollars.
- I can relate in detail my first impressions of my partner.
- I ask my partner about his/her world periodically.
- I feel I know my spouse well.

And if you're not sure whether it's true or false, check it out and actually discuss the items you're not sure about.

Starting to talk about these and other similar questions would be a great way to begin acting like friends again. You can find hundreds of other questions online or in books designed to get couples talking. Take some ideas along on your next date or have them available to use when you get some alone time.

CORNERSTONES OF MARITAL FRIENDSHIP

Let me suggest five of the most essential pieces needed to build or re-build a friendship in your marriage. If you begin or continue to add these to your lifestyle as a couple a little at a time, you will build a strong foundation for your friendship to grow.

TIME TOGETHER

In *Essential 3* I spoke about the importance of margin, leaving room in your life for the truly important. And it's margin that will give you opportunity to make the time to grow as a friendly couple.

My wife Jackie had cancer over ten years ago now and for about eighteen months our life changed dramatically. The day that she was diagnosed we had to begin rearranging our schedule and our time.

Why? Because if we didn't some very bad things were going to happen including the fact that she would probably not live. There was no meeting, no we'll-think-about-it period of time, no consulting with others to determine if we were going to make these changes.

It was a matter of life and death!

Is your marriage worth the same kind of sacrifice, especially to save it or even just to make it way better? I hope so. I know so.

Don't just think about this one. Start today as a couple to plan for and act on what you are going to do or not do to get more time together. Develop segments of your week to be friends and to embrace some of those special friend actions and attitudes that we looked at earlier in this chapter.

It won't matter how many good intentions or practical ideas you have or I give you to connect if you never have time to try them.

Start with building some more margin in your life by getting rid of activities and commitments you can or need to live without.

Next, *put time in your schedule NOW.* Add it to your calendar and do not let some other activity fill those slots you just made available for the two of you. If possible, make it consistent – every Monday, Wednesday night or Sunday afternoon. You won't do this perfectly, no one does, but you will be on your road to time with each other becoming a habit and a precious commodity that you wonder how you did without.

DREAMING

This one is best and most easily a result of your *bucket list* conversations. As you talk about goals or accomplishments that you've always wanted to take on, you need to start dreaming about how you might get there.

Gottman suggests that many marriages get into an ice jam of sorts where their conversations always have an underlying frustration that keeps them from really making progress.

For example, perhaps Alan begins talking about his next job promotion or going back to grad school to help him reach the next leadership plateau at work.

Sharon, his wife, however, has a pit in her stomach and is feeling some anger inside as Alan shares all this with her. He's not doing anything wrong but something has made her irritated and almost bitter.

It's possible that Sharon has had her own dream for a long time of finishing her degree or perhaps working now that the kids are in school. And while she has been happy to put that dream aside she and Alan have never even talked about it.

Some dreaming discussions as two friends could help alleviate her negative attitude and help her to feel understood and ready to work together even if it is still Alan who goes on to school.

Dreaming can also include planning special anniversary trips, living overseas for a year, putting in a pool or buying another house. It could just be going to some concerts together, trying out a new hobby or finally getting to visit that special friend or relative you haven't seen for years.

Dreaming accomplishes many things including feeling heard, having fun, developing new goals and enjoying soul intimacy. Try it.

PLANNING

But if dreaming is going to accomplish anything of note then planning must follow. And I want to say this loud and clear to every married couple:

Half the fun is in the planning!

My wife and I enjoyed a two-month sabbatical recently after seven years of service at the church where I worked. So for many months prior to leaving we began to plan what we were going to do with that two months. We only had so much money but we began to dream.

Since we love to travel we outlined a pretty rigorous, but doable trip first to see our kids, their spouses and our five grandsons. But then we would head west starting in San Francisco, on to Yosemite and then up the coast ending in Seattle.

We had lots of fun putting together an itinerary for both driving and flying, checking out airfares, measuring the distances and seeing where we might go all along the way yet still within our budget.

We had a great plan and were well on our way until . . . our heating and air-conditioning unit went out in our condo. The bill? $5000. We soon realized that our trip was going to have to be shorter and less expensive.

And it was. But it wasn't ruined. We had a great time and still enjoyed San Francisco and the beautiful views in Yosemite. And we still loved the time together to plan. That was half the fun.

Too many men bail on this kind of thing and simply ask their wives to do all the legwork for special activities suggesting their wife just let them know the details later. Bad idea. There is lots of intimacy to be enjoyed in planning things as a team.

And planning isn't just for vacations or more complicated events. Planning is important for a day away, going to a conference together, holiday events or even exploring ideas for teaching or socializing with the children.

BLESSING EACH OTHER

My wife loves to make crafts. I would actually prefer my blood being taken and have absolutely no inherent talent to create something worth keeping anyway. I love languages and have been learning Russian for years. Jackie has no interest in speaking anything other than English and knows maybe five or six words in Russian and Spanish. She will likely learn no more.

Sometimes married people have some very different interests, abilities, hobbies and natural inclinations. But too often couples do not appreciate or even engage in those special leanings and gifts the other has.

Bob may say, "That's Ann's thing so I just get out of the way when she's working on it." Or Ann says, "Sure Bob likes such and such but I just give him his space. I'm not interested."

And while there is good reason for spouses to have certain activities and likes that the other does not do or appreciate, there is still room for blessing one another. What does that mean?

Blessing your spouse means:

You brag about them, even the skills and interests that do not match yours.

You show some interest at times. Because I don't like crafts doesn't mean I don't do anything to encourage and appreciate Jackie's love for them. I don't go to many craft shows but I can listen and enjoy what she shows me and teaches me about them.

In the same way, she takes time to learn about Russia and listen to me speak it even to her at times. We make it fun. She appreciates it when I can translate something for her or speak on her behalf.

You try to at least learn a little bit about the other's passions. Sometimes something the other person enjoys will actually become something we like too. Stay open to that option. Be willing to try or to attend something focused on that interest just to see if there actually is something that also sparks our interest.

You engage with them in that arena at least some of the time. I am so thankful that out of my sixteen trips to Russia Jackie has gone on three of those trips. We've had Russian people in our home, she has learned to cook borscht. There are ways to embrace the other person's loves without becoming an expert.

You affirm them for their uniquenesses. Sometimes we need to literally tell our spouse how much we appreciate and value that they love something, give time to it, are passionate about it and probably help others at times by doing it. We all need affirmation especially from our mate.

ENGAGING SPIRITUALLY

As I discussed in *Essential 2*, intimacy involves body, soul and spirit. So when friendship also includes the spiritual the relationship naturally deepens.

Friends need to be willing to discuss, affirm, question, explore and embrace spiritual issues, actions and attitudes. Go back to the chapter on intimacy and re-read the section on spiritual intimacy. You will quickly see how your friendship can also grow through the spiritual component of your relationship.

Get the idea? Friendship in your marriage must be a normal, natural and developing component of your relationship.

Be sure to spend some time talking about this aspect of your relationship before you move on. Take some small steps to either get started or move forward. As you do you will be convinced more and more that you really did marry your best friend!

DIGGING DEEPER INTO ESSENTIAL 4

1. Talk about some of the friend times you used to enjoy when you were dating or earlier in your marriage. What were they like?

2. Discuss what it would take for you to add more friend time into your relationship. What could you add? What would you delete?

3. Go online and find some other friend questions that you can ask each other during some of your future discussions.

4. Talk about other things you both would enjoy that would be friend-like and fun.

ESSENTIAL 5: LIVE MORE AS WE AND LESS AS ME.

"I will never miss you because of what we do but what we are together."
Nikki Giovanni

A number of years ago I mentioned to Jackie that I was going to go to the office to do some work for a while. Her immediate response was, "Is it work that you could do on the computer here at home?"

I thought for a minute and responded, "Well, sure, but I would be working here just as much as I would be working there." To which she replied, "But it's just different when we're here in the same place."

As a guy it took me some time to understand that but I realized later that, yes, there is something to this *togetherness* thing when two people marry. There is a bond of body, soul and spirit that is more than legal or circumstantial though those things matter.

I saw it vividly again when I was in Russia a few years ago and Jackie was again at home without me. As we talked on the phone she said, "Do you know what I'm missing tonight?" (It was early in the morning for me.)

I said, "No, what are you missing?" She said, "I'm missing watching television with your legs on my lap." You see, that's pretty much our routine after about five minutes of viewing a favorite program or movie. I'll turn a little sideways and put my legs on her lap.

She likes that and so do I. It's a form of togetherness for us.

Togetherness is a *deep understanding that while we are unique individuals there is a physical, emotional and spiritual closeness that we both enjoy and need as a married couple.*

Togetherness is not about losing one's identity or personhood. As I discussed in an earlier chapter, men and women always have unique interests, personalities and preferences but in marriage they must still embrace, enjoy and celebrate a togetherness that is distinctly for married people.

And of course, togetherness is not exclusive to marriage but it is central to marriage in a unique form that cannot be replicated anywhere else. And yet so many couples do not understand its role and importance. They still think more about ME than WE.

You would think they met on *MEharmony.com* not *eharmony.com*!

Some avoid togetherness because of *ignorance*. No one ever taught them how to both intimately connect with another person without losing who they are. Others simply *think marriage is mostly about sex* and living together, throwing a couple of kids in the mix for fun.

Others are *selfish* and don't understand that love is about being willing to give up some of your own personal independence and freedom so that you can share a dual dependence that results in a new freedom.

Whatever the reasons, healthy couples must learn that *they can be better together than separate* but to do so will require understanding togetherness. A classic marriage maxim says this: *Don't try to find someone to marry you can live with. Find someone you can't live without.*

My hunch is that if more people went into marriage with that thought in their journey to their wedding day there would be little concern about togetherness. They would quickly start thinking as we instead of me.

SO WHAT MIGHT **WE LIVING** LOOK LIKE IN A MARRIAGE?

I am going to suggest in the *Digging Deeper* ideas at the end of this chapter that you and your spouse determine specific problem or growth areas for your relationship. There would be too many possibilities for me to cover in a chapter of a book.

Nonetheless, let me provide you with some key WE situations that I've seen couples struggle with most during my years of counseling.

Decision-making. Too many spouses assume that they are the expert when it comes to key decisions in certain areas. Many of those choices to be made revolve around finances, buying real estate, using the computer, major purchases or a host of other things.

For example, the couple has talked about a new home, selling theirs and trying to make a little money in the process. John, who has a real estate background, assumes that his wife Sheila really can't bring much expertise at all to their search so he charges ahead.

And Sheila as a result feels hurt. She should. Why? Because marriage is about WE more than ME.

While one of you, like John in this case, may actually be more *experienced* in some area, that doesn't mean that you suddenly become the one to make the final decision without input from the other person.

When spouses don't consider the perspective of the other they can intentionally or perhaps more often unintentionally send the message that the other is stupid, uninformed or without a helpful perspective or opinion. In reality making one's own decision no matter how much experience or background you have is the foolish choice.

Making decisions as a team is an important way to build *respect* and *add value to one another.* The contrary is also true. When we make a huge decision without talking it over with our spouse we say to them, *"Your opinion doesn't matter. You are not intelligent enough for me to consult with you."*

Hardly a way to increase intimacy, is it?

SILOS

Having lived in rural areas for many of my adult years I've seen a lot of farms and their ubiquitous silos. I even used to work out in a climbing gym that was set up in a huge silo in the middle of Illinois.

Silos of course are generally used to store grain and often stand alone in a field somewhere boldly pointing toward the empty sky.

Interestingly, couples often develop their own silos that can add to a lack of WE or genuine togetherness in their marriage. I've implied a few in the previous chapters but let me highlight several more.

There can be *financial silos*. Each person has a job and their own bank accounts. The couple treats the money they make as generally *their money*, not our money, and they only share it if they want to. And while there can be a place for separate accounts (i.e. a business account), total separation of finances makes a strong statement that you don't understand the importance of a WE relationship yet.

It should not matter who makes the most income or what the money is for. In a WE marriage, it all belongs to both of you and should be treated that way.

We can build *time silos*. "This is my time, my hobby, my room to veg out in, my need for space, etc." And again while couples do require and need time for themselves, that's another decision that should be discussed first and then modeled by both partners agreeing that the decision is wise for them and their marriage.

In fact it is often a misuse or overuse of personal time that steals important moments that couples should have together.

We can develop *work and career silos*. My wife's dad was a pastor for fifty years before he died. And while he and Joyce didn't have a perfect home Jackie rarely felt the angst that many pastors' kids feel when their dads frequently change jobs, face the stress of people who need them all the time and have to move around a lot.

So I asked her one time why her adjustments living in a pastor's home were so minimal and she answered quickly, "Because my dad never treated his ministry as only his. We all were a part of the process and the decisions."

Many husbands and wives look the other way when one or the other gets a career-building opportunity. It's just assumed that they will move or one of them will travel four days a week or that they will have fewer meals or activities that they enjoy together. The decision is made and everyone lives with it.

You see any of these and other silos steal togetherness from us as a couple and make the marriage more about ME than WE. Admit your silos and slowly start to rearrange your life and tear them down.

Personal hobbies and accomplishment. Most people have things they like to do that the other person does not. Today those hobbies or unique interests often include: *sports, crafts, working with one's hands, reading, cycling, music and exercise*, just to name a few.

However, these extracurricular activities often turn into obsessive behaviors and commitments that soon begin draining significant time, money and emotional resources from their relationship and ultimately the interactions of the whole family when children are involved.

Decisions about the amount of time either of you spend on hobbies and the like must also be on the agenda for discussion and ultimately make a wise decision about how you will proceed. You need to evaluate those choices based on their impact on your parenting, health, finances and personal time.

Is giving the kind of time you're sacrificing to each endeavor worth the risk and the payoff? Can you still enjoy that pastime even if you cut back on your involvement?

Discipline and childrearing. Ben and Suzanne grew up in very different homes. Ben's parents were extremely strict, rarely put up with any roughhousing and handed out spankings and punishments like they were pennies.

Suzanne's parents, however, were more middle of the road. They had clear guidelines but made room for exceptions and treated disrespect and poor behavior with firmness, not corporal punishment.

However, a couple years after their wedding date Ben and Suzanne became parents. Of course they loved that new little guy who looked at them with adoring eyes, cooed when they played and laughed out loud. They wanted to hug and kiss him every day.

Until he turned two.

Then they realized that precious little Cade was slowly turning into a monster. Well, not really, but all of a sudden they possessed a child who had his own way of doing things and didn't always obey. He fussed, cried and whined when things didn't fit his liking.

He had a mind of his own and was proud of it.

And Rob and Suzanne *both* thought they knew the best way to rein Cade in. Unfortunately, they weren't on the same page as to how to do it.

Instead they each believed with all their hearts that their way of responding, which was actually closest to their parents' form of discipline, was *the* way to handle him. Often they would just act or react and think little of their spouse's position.

And when parents are not on the same page, the kids become confused and unsure of who to follow. And the kids usually win if they cannot decide *together* how to discipline their children.

Great parents are WE parents who decide ahead of time what the key components and parameters of their parenting will be even if that means compromising and re-thinking some of the concepts they learned in their own home growing up.

What are the biggest discipline problems in your home right now? Talk them over with your spouse and determine what you are both going to do to limit those problems in your house. Be WE instead of ME and discuss how you will turn your discipline into a united front rather than a disjointed and inconsistent mess.

But whatever you do, *do not just assume* that your way is best. Let your spouse bring their insights and helps to the table so that you both can do a better and more effective job of raising your kids well. Read my book *Turn Up or Turn Around Your Parenting* for more practical help and ideas.

Goal setting. It is interesting that CEO's and their leadership teams set goals, non-profits set goals, sports teams and coaches set goals and yet very few families ever do. And the few that do set them often let the goal setting be led by one spouse or the other.

In addition, those goals are often focused on the temporal things – finances, retirement, college, promotions and places to live. And while those things are important and should receive attention and planning, there are greater goals a husband and wife need to consider *together*.

Leadership expert and author Patrick Lencioni suggests that we should look at goals the way a healthy organization considers them. For example, every organization must scale down their efforts and main attention to first this question: *What is the core purpose of your being a family?* That should be followed with the *three or so values* that you will keep at the forefront of your home as you live out that purpose.

Determine next *what you actually do* in your home to make that happen. After that decide *what makes your home different* from others (compared to what's called your *competition* in the business world).

Next, determine what is your biggest priority *right now* that you need to shore up to stay on track. Finally, who is responsible for carrying out the tasks that need to be done?

So you see there is much fertile ground for the establishment of a WE mentality in your marriage but it will take fertilizing, weeding and other regular attention to bear fruit in these and other areas of your marriage.

Work at it, make it a high priority and start somewhere to take your next step.

TOO MUCH TOGETHERNESS?

It is possible to go to the other extreme, however, and overdo it on togetherness to the point of smothering each other and not letting your relationship and individuality breathe a little. This often is compounded when one or both partners have latent fears of being abandoned, don't trust the other person for some reason or are naturally jealous.

If any of the following actions or habits are regularly occurring in one or both of you consider getting some counseling help to look at deeper issues and concerns:

Demands that the other person "check in" an unreasonable amount of times each day.

One person checking the other's phone, email and texts all the time.

Rarely allowing the other person any alone time with friends or at home.

One spouse having no close friends of their own.

Nagging the other about being gone even now and then when their absences are actually reasonable and normal.

When almost all social activity is only with each other or each other's family members.

While demanding *togetherness* may appear like a WE issue, it's usually about ME because it's being demanded, carried to an unhealthy extreme and often devious.

So how is your marriage doing on the WE vs. ME front? Most of us, if we're honest, will likely need to do some work to get away from the ME arenas that aren't helpful, productive or intimacy-producing.

Use the Digging Deeper questions to get you started. It will take time to develop a newer, healthier culture that still celebrates your uniqueness but brings you together more intimately in every area of life. Give it time but start now to make changes. It's likely there are a lot of great moments and experiences ahead of you... *together*.

DIGGING DEEPER INTO ESSENTIAL 5

1. Think about and admit areas where YOU have had more of a ME attitude and perspective than a WE one. Ask forgiveness if necessary for not including your spouse more in that area.

2. After developing each of your lists, decide on one or two areas where you will start acting and thinking together, making decisions with each other and becoming one more of the time.

3. Spend some time praying that you and your spouse will do the hard work to take the first or next steps in having a togetherness mindset in these areas.

4. Talk about those individual interests, goals and activities that you will still celebrate and encourage the other to do. Is there a need to cut back or re-think any of those?

ESSENTIAL 6: COMMUNICATE FROM THE HEART

"He who answers before listening – that is his folly and his shame."
*– **Proverbs 18:13***

Cal and Ginny were screaming at each other. No, their conversation had not started that way. It never did. They had initially disagreed on how much money they were going to spend on their next vacation. Ginny thought they should be more frugal this year, but Cal was adamant they could afford more.

He argued that it had been a tough year and that they all could use some R&R. The last thing they needed was to cut back on a remedy for their exhaustion and ragged nerves.

She on the other hand mentioned their growing debt, a rather significant amount, and that she did not want to add to it. In fact, Ginny reminded him that they had told their financial advisor that they would pay down what they owed and not add to it under any circumstances.

But as their opinions collided over the next twenty minutes they also observed their personhoods smashing into each other. Ginny began to suggest to Cal that he was the one who got them into all this debt in the first place while Cal told her that she was again being *Debbie Downer* and a spoil sport. In his mind her frugality was ruining their ability to be a normal family and to just have fun.

And as their cutting words tore through each other's hearts and the pain ramped up as a result, their anger skyrocketed and it was hard to stop yelling.

How did they get here? Why did a simple disagreement become like the next world war? How could two people who love each other, who promised to always cherish and build up their spouse now be screaming at the person they promised to spend the rest of their lives with?

Well, it's likely that it started back at *Essential 1* within their *mistaken identity.* Cal and Ginny are still fighting for their worth as a person. They both want to be right, not look bad or appear stupid and have gone to war to win a battle that really isn't a fatal one. They just think it is.

So fundamentally if they are going to communicate and even argue effectively they must start by being reminded that even if their spouse is adamantly opposed to them for the moment or sees some major fault in them, their value has not been diminished one iota. In God's eyes, they are still His child, matter to Him, have purpose, are forgiven and loved.

And once they understand that then they can more freely speak to their spouse from the heart and listen without having to defend or protect.

I would suggest that before you read on in this chapter that you go back and review *Essential 1* again. Make sure your worth, value and personhood are standing on what God thinks of you not your spouse's thoughts at any given moment. *No person can ever say or do enough for us to give us 100% satisfaction regarding our worth or value.*

There is no such thing as human unconditional love. Human compassions can be good, even great, but not perfect. Only God's love is unconditional. That must be our standard. And if it is then we will be more ready and willing to communicate with our spouse from the heart, not just the head, and enter into deeper conversations about differences, perspective and everyday challenges.

BARRIERS TO HEART COMMUNICATION

Unfortunately, several common actions and attitudes by spouses in a marriage hamstring intimacy and impacting conversations. Gottman again summarizes them in what he calls *The Four Horsemen.*

Criticism. Some people can hardly say anything without finding fault. The other person is never good enough and God forbid they make a mistake. Constant criticism tears away at the heart of the other person and makes it hard to ever share anything meaningful, even when it's something good.

Defensiveness. Some people always have an excuse for their actions even when they are clearly wrong or unwise. Defensive people rarely listen, engage in helpful discussions for making things better or learn from their mistakes. And they kill heart communication.

Stonewalling. Others like to use the silent treatment, especially men. For some this can be a nice, *acceptable way* to avoid conflict but never really deal with the issues below the surface. I used to do this one a lot. A husband once asked if I was a witch or something because I began to tell him how I was sure he related to his wife.

He then asked me if I had some kind of witch-like powers! But I simply told him that I too had been just like him. My wife and I would have a disagreement before I left for work. And some of the struggle involved my poor actions.

However, rather than deal with it I'd just come home, grab the paper and turn on the television hoping there would be no more discussion about it and all would be forgotten.

Contempt. If there is one of the four that is the worst this is it. Contempt is when one person speaks *words of death* (see *Essential 2*) or acts in such a way that they attack the character and personhood of the other. Their response is typically demeaning, hurtful and unkind and can be expressed or seen even in an expression or tone of voice.

But remember for now that healthy communication strategies and methods which we'll highlight next can only work when two things pave the way: *Both spouses must understand where their true identify resides and be committed to avoiding the Four Horsemen.*

SO HOW DOES COMMUNICATION OF THE HEART HAPPEN?

First, it requires that we go *beneath the surface.* Gary Smalley has suggested that there are at least five key levels of communication from shallow to deeper. The diagram below lists them.

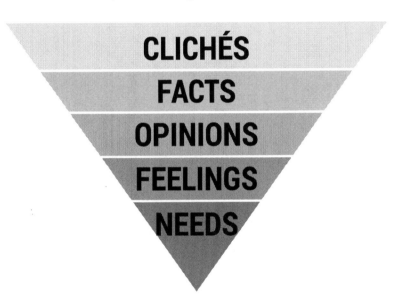

The most shallow is obviously clichés. Then we come to *facts* and *opinions.* Facts are important as they lay the groundwork for our discussions and make sure we're talking about the same things and with accuracy.

If, for example, a couple is fighting about money but forgets the *fact* that they have two extra bank accounts that they have neglected to include in their discussion their fight will be over nothing and at best misguided.

But we must also get beyond *opinions.* In fact, opinions are where we typically fight. "I think we're spending too much money," one says. The other responds, "No we're not. You just spent hundreds on a television last week. Why are we suddenly becoming frugal today?"

Because our worth is on the line and our identity is skewed we go to war on the opinion level. We don't want to look stupid, feel small, be deemed as inadequate or incompetent. And this is where the *Four Horsemen* often rear up and get used as our *protection from further damage to our fragile personhood.*

If our communication is going to be meaningful and from the heart, if we are going to obtain true soul intimacy, we must also talk about our *feelings and needs.*

Feelings are unfortunately often expressed as disguised opinions. "I feel that you never listen," or "I feel that we need to move," are just opinions with the word feel in them.

Real feelings have a feeling word in them: *angry, disappointed, hurt, sad, overwhelmed, confused, bitter.* It will actually take some practice for to learn to use those richer, more helpful and accurate words.

But feelings are usually what are behind or beneath our opinions. For example, if a wife is arguing about overspending there's a good chance that she is worried, even fearful, of not having enough money to pay all the bills because money is tight.

If a husband thinks his wife is nagging him about looking for work, he may be feeling overwhelmed or embarrassed that he's not providing for the family. Couples who communicate well are willing to explore one another's feelings about what is going on in their lives.

They aren't likely psychotherapists or counselors and do not have to be. One of the best things we can do is *wonder* a lot. "Honey, I wonder if you're not really confused right now." Or, "It seems to me that you're pretty angry because of what happened last night." You guess, explore and ponder with each other until you come up with just the right word or words that best express the other's true feelings.

When you get there, to the real feeling deep within, you will know it. There will be an obvious lump in the throat or tear in the eye of the other person or perhaps a profound quietness.

But getting to that feeling level is essential to intimacy. Each of you will, if nothing else, feel like you have been understood. That's half the battle. In fact, often for women it's 90% of the battle. They often want their husbands to know, "I just need to be understood. Please!"

Do not rush this stage and do not settle for a feeling that isn't really what either one of you feels. For example, don't settle for angry when you're really bitter. Don't settle for tired when you're really overwhelmed. Finding the right feeling is a little like an archaeologist trying to find a lost artifact.

They have to go slowly, work their way around what is good and be very careful to protect their discovery. Using a big pick isn't what's needed if a small brush or file will do. But that means you need to take time with each other's feelings. They are delicate.

And *stay away from generic words.* Being *frustrated* for example doesn't tell you much of anything. Get to the real deal.

THE DEEPEST LEVEL

Once the feelings are discussed and confirmed, then you should talk about *needs.* After John has discovered the real reason his wife is feeling what she does about their money problems, he might say something like this:

"Mary, what do you need from me that would help you feel less anxious and worried about our finances?" Or Marty might reply to her husband, "Alan, what do you need from me that would lessen your feeling defeated around the rest of the family?"

This is where you move toward very real change and actions. *You are committing to not just expressing your concerns but actually doing something about them.*

Discovering needs will probably require some additional *clarification, compromise and understanding* but it's worth the effort. You won't be perfect at your new communication skills but you can start. And then the two of you must put feet to your commitment to actually care enough to change your actions the next time and better meet their need.

It will also be important that the two of you periodically evaluate how you're doing and whether more changes or discussion are needed.

At first, this whole feelings and needs process will feel awkward and even forced but if you work at it so that it becomes a natural part of how you speak to each other you will find yourself arguing less and actually accomplishing more even through your conflict.

A FEW OTHER IMPORTANT COMMUNICATION GUIDELINES AND PRINCIPLES

There are three words that every conversation, especially those in conflict, must include. Those words are *Here and Now.*

So often our conversations revert to the past through some event or circumstance that occurred in the present. For example, you feel like your wife didn't really hear what you said and made a mountain out of a molehill.

As a result, your response to her was, "You never listen, do you? It's always all about you when we discuss this. I wish you would just one time hear what I have to say in its entirety before you respond so vehemently."

That's not a here and now statement. It includes the past and in some ways is predicting the future. When we don't limit our responses to the here and now, we start to use terms like *never and always*. We may call the other names or compare them to a parent. All of these comments stray away from *the current issues* and are ultimately ineffective, cruel and even contemptuous.

A better response would be, "I'm irritated right now because it seems like you're not listening to me very much." (*Feeling statement*). Do you see the difference? Here and now only deals with what is happening at the moment or in the present.

Effective connecting between spouses does not use the past to bash, manipulate or harm. It only speaks of what is happening or just happened. "It hurt me last night when you make a joke about me in front of our friends," is a here and now statement as opposed to, "You always try to make me look bad when we're around other people."

In reality comments like these are really *words of death* that I referenced in an earlier chapter. When we limit our comments to the here and now we actually move ourselves back into line for more words of life.

And when we stay current it's far easier to move to the *needs* step and talk about what could have been or could be different.

TIMING MATTERS

Great communication is like cooking a wonderful steak. Timing counts and you can't rush it. Both partners need to be sensitive to what else is going on around them and in the other person as they try to communicate from the heart.

Starting a deep conversation, for example, on the way to church or a wedding or your nephew's graduation probably isn't the right time. Only leaving yourselves thirty minutes to handle a gritty topic or struggle is unwise.

Sometimes you'll need to stop because it's 1:00am and neither of you has any more energy or cogent thinking capacity to move forward. You can always make a *commitment for more* the next morning or evening.

WHAT YOU SEE CAN BE WHAT YOU GET

For decades now researchers have studied the impact of body language on communication and agree on at least one thing: *What we see in the other person also matters when we interact*. Because most of us are very visual creatures anyway, something as small as an expression, position of the hands or arms and how we're seated can derail a meaningful and potentially helpful discussion.

Often when I ask couple to interact with each other in my office, one of them will literally need to turn around because their body has been distinctively turned away from their spouse.

So to help avoid physical distractions we need to make sure we: *look at the other person without staring, face them at least in part and move relatively close to them without it feeling awkward*. We also need to turn off the television, step away from our computer or put down our smartphone.

LISTENING

Remember the phrase one of my counseling mentors used to say, "Listen beneath the words?" There are some practical things you can do to improve your ability to listen well, something essential to great communication from the heart.

First, literally practice repeating *the other's comments almost word for word including their feeling word*. "So, Allison, you're angry because this morning I suggested we would go out to eat as a family and then I just changed my mind in the last minute?" At first it will sound almost mechanical but start there until you become freer to make your comments more your own.

Don't be afraid to *stop the other person often and summarize*. Focus on their feeling and why they feel that way before letting them go on to more detail. This is the time to clarify their feeling and make sure you've landed on the best word.

Second, if there are any obvious distractions, *acknowledge and correct them*. "I'm going to need to turn the television off so I can hear better and concentrate more on what you're saying."

You see communicating from the heart or soul takes work. It's potentially uncomfortable but it's one of the key gateways to real intimacy. And whether you and your spouse are good at it or not isn't the question.

The question is, *"Will you begin to expose the deep recesses of your own heart to the other and embrace the exposed soul of your spouse, treating it with tenderness, understanding, a listening ear and compassion?"*

You can. Get started today.

DIGGING DEEPER INTO ESSENTIAL 6

1. What things are most significantly hindering your communication as spouses?

2. What could you do right now to give yourselves more time to talk?

3. What feelings have each of you felt most strongly recently that you've not shared with each other?

4. What would you be willing to do so that your spouse would not feel some of their negative feelings so strongly.

ESSENTIAL 7: LIVE **TODAY** NOT SOMEDAY.

"What day is it?" "It's today," squeaked Piglet. "My favorite day," said Pooh.
– A.A. Milne

When is the last time you or your spouse said something like, "You know, someday we need to _____."

You might have filled in the blank with...*take a special trip together, go back to school, serve at the church, help with a missions project, start having more time off, save for retirement, go back to school, spend more family time with the kids, get into a small group, go on a unique vacation, lose weight* or one of a hundred more possibilities.

But most of those ideas have given way to seemingly more urgent day- to-day responsibilities, habits and obligations, haven't they? The everyday things of life have intentionally or unintentionally been allowed to fill and even manage your lives.

In *Essential 3* I talked about the importance of adding margin to our lives, making room for some of those someday hopes to become reality now. And margin is certainly one of the key components of living in the present more than the future.

I hope you've already been thinking about how to add some important space to the busyness of your life.

However, I think many of us are caught in something I like to call the *Someday Syndrome*. We believe that there are lots of things we need to be doing, enjoying, changing and embracing but they must all wait for *someday*.

Why?

Because we have other things we must do now and all the rest can wait. And for many couples someday includes their marriage getting better.

So in this chapter I want to explore some other concepts beyond adding margin that can either keep you stuck or help you move forward to make your marriage all that it can be.

They can give you the perspective and tools you need to get out of the *Someday Syndrome* and instead started on some actual significant change and growth.

THE POWER OF INERTIA.

When I was MUCH younger I rode a bicycle across the country with a group of friends from college. It was an awesome, exhausting and life-changing kind of trip with many more details and stories to tell than I can include here.

However, early in the trip while we were descending from the mountains out west, I learned a lot about the power of inertia.

We were riding in groups of six and had been told that we were going to have an eleven–mile coast. Therefore, we couldn't be riding close together but would have to spread out and ride this section on our own.

And so each of us would push off from the top of the pass, slowly approach the steepness of the decline and immediately begin to feel the pull of gravity. It was a wild ride where at times we were reaching speeds of fifty miles per hour and more.

While gravity was dictating our increase in speed, inertia was coming into play again.

When our bikes were standing still it took some effort to get the bike moving. Inertia is first of all the *tendency of an object standing still to stay standing still.* Many marriages are stalled and going nowhere because of that form of inertia.

Inertia was also felt however when I tried to stop or slow down. Inertia in concert with gravity made us go faster and faster causing us to also use our brakes a lot so that we would not fall or crash. Inertia is also that *tendency for an object that is moving to keep moving.*

Inertia is typically a factor in marriages, both good and bad, especially when it comes to living in the someday.

One of the reasons we don't grow in our marriages and do the things that we know would enhance, strengthen and enrich our relationship is because of that first kind of inertia. We're sort of happy with where we are, it's easier to just keep doing what we're doing and to get started with a new venture just seems like too much effort.

We don't really want to push that hard or give the kind of energy it will take to get moving again.

Don't succumb to inertial paralysis if you want to turn up or turn around your marriage!

Overcoming this first type of inertia in a marriage will require some significant extra force or energy to get started. It may mean taking a first step or two towards one of your goals.

For example, if you and your spouse know you need to spend more time together then you will probably need to make some initial choices about things you may need to cut and what you're going to add to help you find time together.

Start small but start somewhere. Do not wait any longer. Be on the same page, talk about your initial goal and do it. If you have children let them in on it depending upon their age of course. But you will be teaching your kinds some important lessons about marriage as well as you show them how you are making each other a priority.

And once you get moving, the second inertia kicks in where you find it's not that hard to keep going in the same direction. You take that first special trip and realize how refreshing and refilling it was. You begin putting a small amount of time together each week and discover that you are already looking forward to the next time.

Use emotional physics, *the law of inertia*, to help ramp up and enrich your marriage.

THE POWER OF PRIORITIES

Another reason couples don't make changes and improvements today is because they haven't made growing their relationship a priority. Work, kids, money, clubs, hobbies and the like have all helped use up the hours in their family schedule.

They think, "This is a lot to worry about right now. I can't add anything else. Besides, these are my children and I want to give them the best of my time and energies."

And while most things that take the bulk of our time are not bad, they are not always best. They aren't enhancing our relationship, growing our friendship with each other, pointing us closer to God or helping us live life to the fullest. *They can cause us to feel more like we're just existing, not living.*

So at some point we have to *decide* that we're not only going to make changes but that they are important, vital ones and not optional any more.

I'm hoping that you've already been challenged about some of those priorities by reading the earlier chapters and essentials. The study questions were designed to get you thinking so hopefully you're already in process.

But if they still aren't a high enough priority then you will likely keep thinking about them but won't actually do them now. *You will remain stuck in the someday.*

So how can you prioritize and move forward?

First, *take some time away as a couple and talk with each other and God about your marriage and family.* Have you ever considered what the major reasons are for your family being in existence? Have you ever talked about what God may have uniquely called you to do and be?

And no, I'm not suggesting that you need to think about the mission field though be open to that. I am suggesting that you need to figure out with God's help what you will give the bulk of your time, energy, money and other resources to.

It will involve looking more specifically how you spend your days, what you want your kids to really learn, considering the things that you think are important while everyone is still in your home.

What are the three values that you believe need to guide everything you do and those that you have already let direct you that may need to change?

For example, maybe you believe that *hard work* is a value in your home. Is it? Or that *time together* is important. Does that happen? What are the top things that you will not budge on no matter what? These exercises and times of discussion together about them will help you make the tough decisions that will keep you living today and not someday.

In his excellent management and leadership book, *The Advantage*,

Patrick Lencioni tells the story of Southwest Airlines and how one of their *values to die* for is their use of humor.

However, apparently a person was upset that the employees would use humor even during the safety instructions. So she wrote to the president of Southwest and and suggested she was offended at the practice and that she would not be flying Southwest anymore.

To which the president wrote back a three-word letter. *We'll miss you*. We need to be that serious about our priorities and values in our homes and marriages.

Determine what's most important NOW and stick to it.

THE POWER OF CONSEQUENCES

About the time we were married, Jackie and I were privileged to know and serve in a church and school led by a wonderful pastor nearing retirement. He was beloved by so many and while people were sad that he was ending his regular ministry in the church they were happy for him and his wife.

They spoke of the travel and other trips with family that they would enjoy during their retirement years. There was just one problem. He died within the next year.

How sad to have looked forward to those special times only to see them flitter away through unexpected death.

I don't want to be overly morbid here but one of the consequences of putting off our todays to someday is that we may never get to enjoy our somedays. Bad things happen, circumstances change. Like this godly pastor, the someday may never come. We need to anticipate what we could possibly miss out on by waiting.

While we can't do everything we want now, *we can do some things*. Literally ponder the consequences of waiting and then not reaching your goal.

But there are other potential losses that can come from waiting. *Age may keep us from enjoying something later in the way we could now.* Yes, we should try to stay healthy and fit, but sometimes that is not an option.

Our walking, traveling and mental capacities may not be quite the same.

Our *marriage could continue to suffer* or deteriorate to the point where there is no hope by the time *someday* rolls around. We can't assume things will just get better as time goes on. Our relationship may seriously need attention that only some conscious today living and change can provide.

Other consequences? *Regret, disappointment, wasted time and money, lack of fulfillment, missed opportunities for our family.*

Only you can decide what you will focus on and when. But as leadership guru Seth Godin says, *"You don't need more time. You just need to decide."*

THE POWER OF DECIDING

Please decide now that you are going to work on your marriage, shore up your priorities and take some first steps in the right direction. You don't need more time. You need to act. My hunch is that this book hasn't been your first nudge or even push to move forward.

Perhaps you've been to counseling, heard challenges from your pastors, had talks with your spouse, been encouraged by friends, read other books or articles, been to a seminar or done several or all of the above.

It's possible that the missing element has not been that you don't know what to do, though we can always learn more. *You just haven't done what you need to do.* You've blamed each other, the schedule, God, time limits or whatever when the problem is simply you've not acted on your knowledge.

Mere knowledge is only knowledge. *Knowledge acted upon is wisdom.* So do not let this chapter close and read through a few more good ideas in the appendix-like final chapter without a prayerful commitment to actually take action NOW.

Cross the line in the sand and say, "We're not going back or staying the same." We are going to turn up and turn around this marriage. We're all in. We are not going to live in the someday anymore. Today we start living TODAY.

I promise you if you make a decision like that and then begin to act on it now, God will also be *all in* with you and help your marriage and family to be more and better than it's ever been.

DIGGING DEEPER INTO ESSENTIAL 7

1. Plan a time away to do the exercises suggested in this chapter to get you started on making changes NOW.

2. If you haven't already, put your first schedule/activity change on the calendar and begin to anticipate it.

3. Talk about any fears that you have about making these changes or trying new things. Use the guidelines in the last chapter to help you share and listen well.

EXTRA MARRIAGE BUILDERS

As a little bonus I'm throwing in a few other marriage boosters that we have done or tried over the years that seemed like keepers. They may work for you or may not. Pick and choose but try them when you've run out of ideas or just want to get adventurous.

Some are better than others. Some require extra expense and planning. Others you can do spur of the moment.

Whatever you do, have fun, make memories and even come up with some ideas on your own that this list inspired.

READING TO ONE ANOTHER IN THE CAR

Even though you could do this one using pre-recorded books played through your car audio system, consider actually reading a book to each other out loud while you're travelling.

Of course this depends upon who's driving and who else is in the car but there is something special and personal about actually reading it yourself. You can easily stop, for example, and talk about a certain concept or perspective.

Reading on your own allows you to go at your own pace and it keeps you both a bit more involved. Of course you can include fiction but I'm specifically thinking of reading books together that might help your relationship and intimacy.

ROMANTIC DATES

There are a number of books, CD's and articles out there to provide ideas but the general premise is my focus here. Often our *romance* gets a bit boring because we don't put much creativity into what happens before, during and after.

So a little creativity and attention can spice things up. Using the books or your own imagination you each take turns coming up with the romantic date details. They often include dinner, some change in location or atmosphere and guarded time for you both alone.

If you use an outside resource make sure that the ideas are ones that you both are willing to try and feel comfortable doing. You'll figure that out pretty quickly and can always skip those that don't suit your lifestyle, preferences or comfort levels.

The timeframe is up to you, too. Once a week, once a month? You decide. You can also have a financial guideline and most ideas have options that you can choose from that help you control costs, travel and time constraints.

SPECIAL ANNIVERSARY TRIPS

We did not start these until well into our marriage but they have become a real highlight and something we now look forward to both planning and enjoying every five years or so.

The concept is pretty easy. Every five years we plan a trip that is a bit more special, costly and involved to celebrate our latest marriage plateau.

As I alluded to in the book, the planning is one of the best parts so each of you should be involved. Yes, each partner might take on a certain portion of the research but both of you must engage in the details of making it happen and determining where you will go.

Start with a list of reasonable options and narrow down your choices for the next significant anniversary. Do your research, share notes and then decide. At this point you should still be a year or more out and have started saving, making reservations and determining the details of where you will go.

You might want to join a tour or just do things on your own. That will likely determine the amount of work for you but it's your call. For one of our recent trips, we decided on a cruise/land tour to Alaska so they worked on many of the basic details for us.

However, because it was both a cruise and land tour we were able to pick many of the specific things we would do along the way. We like having both some structure and freedom. *Do what works for you.*

I can tell you this. Some of our most enjoyable times in marriage were not just the trips themselves, though they have been wonderful, but the planning, researching and trying to find great deals. We've had a blast pulling these trips together and hope to do several more.

PROMISES FOR MORE

This little way of responding can be used in a number of scenarios. The problem is that sometimes we have to turn each other down. It may be that we're too tired or sick for sex or that we simply do not have the energy, time or presence of mind to have a long discussion.

Sometimes I've been at the office all day talking to people and Jackie wants to talk about something when I get home. And she deserves my time and attention even more than those who I deal with at work. But I don't want to give her a less than helpful or cogent mind so I'll offer her a *promise for more*.

I might say, "*Jackie, I'm willing to talk right now but I may not have much mind and heart power left to be of much help. Can we wait and talk in the morning? I'll stay home away from work until we're finished.*"

The idea is that we let our spouse know after our rejection that we're not saying "no" because of something they did wrong or for any other questionable motive. We want them to know that time with them matters but that we cannot give our best right now. So we make a promise for more.

When it came to sex, we would suggest to one another that we could have a "date" the next night or whatever. In that context the word *date* did not refer to dinner and a movie! We were committing to be romantic and offering a promise for more. Get it?

MISSIONS/SERVING OPPORTUNITIES TOGETHER

I alluded in *Essential 2* that spiritual intimacy is often grown in the context of serving together. So I won't add a lot more here other than to suggest a few more ideas.

You can serve at church, at a non-profit, in your neighborhood, through a local ministry or yes on a missions trip. The key is that at least some of the time you go together. Because when the two of you serve the two of you have *intimate* things to talk about, common experiences and things to look forward to in the future.

And yes there is a place for father/daughter, mother/son and kids only trips but make sure that you and your spouse make going together a priority, too.

ANNUAL GETAWAYS/EVALUATIONS

Of course our children get report cards, employees get annual reviews and athletes get grades and scores.

But how many marriages ever receive an evaluation? Far too few. And the best person to do that evaluation is YOU!

We tried to find at least one opportunity each year to get away for both some fun and to look back at the last year of our relationship. We would typically try to answer two questions: One was, *How did we do as a couple this past year?* And two, *What do we want to do better this next year?*

I would suggest that you develop some key categories that you look at such as: *communication, relating to the children, planning, priorities and finances*. However, make up your own list, one that gets you to the core of your marriage.

Spend some time talking about both the plusses and the minuses. Write your findings down. Then start deciding what you will do this year to shore up some of those weak areas. You can then use this list the following year as your guide for discussion and future improvement.

And if you have trouble finding the time to get away, you might consider adding a few days to a business trip one of you has.

THE BUCKET LIST

Of course the term *bucket list* became popular by a movie of the same name but it simply involves a person or couple listing special things they want to do before they *kick the bucket (die)*.

And while that may sound gruesome to some it can actually be a fun activity that helps couples plan to do things together that they might tend to wait to do later. Remember the *Someday Syndrome*?

I was a pastor in various churches and continue in ministry because of a time when Jackie and I got away and talked about things we've always wanted to do but had not done. One of the items on my list was going to seminary. And over the next several years I did just that at a seminary some 1200 miles from where we lived.

It was quite a challenge but we worked on it together and had a great time figuring out how to make it work. It became our *project* not just mine.

THE FAVORITES GAME

This is another simple and fun way to connect with your spouse especially if you have not had much together time of late. (Works with children, too!) Each of you picks a category and then you try to guess the other's favorite in that category – i.e. ice cream, fast food, dream trip, color, recent vacation, TV show, book read, etc.

Take turns and keep it fun. It could however lead to some deeper discussions reserved for another extended time.

PRAYING WHILE STAYING AWAKE

Over the years Jackie and I have tried many different options for praying together on a regular basis. Some worked well, some did not. We're not one of those couples who naturally have a time we pray together though we value prayer both separately and as a couple.

However, for a time we tried praying together before we went to sleep. The problem was that much of the time while Jackie was praying I literally went to sleep.

So we incorporated something that was at one time called *conversational prayer.* And it's a great method no matter what time of day or night you try to use it plus it helps keep people like me awake.

One person starts a topic or time of praise with their prayer not praying long or continuing to a new topic until the other person has had a chance to jump in if they so desire. And now when we're home together and pray before we eat, we both pray.

TRADITIONS

Establish some of your own traditions for just the two of you. Could you regularly go to a favorite restaurant, return to a special vacation place or always celebrate your anniversary (or even one ending in '5" or '0') in an extra special way?

Is there a conference that one of you attends each year that your spouse could tag along on and you then extend your stay? Do you always spend New Year's Eve doing something just for the two of you or attend the opening night of every *Star Wars* sequel.

Figure out some fun and meaningful traditions that just include you without the kids.

COMMON PASSIONS

Too many couples spend lots of time and resources on their own hobbies, interests and goals but leave very little energy for some you can do together that don't necessarily involve the kids. We enjoy hiking, traveling, reading to mention just a few.

But we maximize those and make sure that most weeks include some time together doing things we both enjoy. Serving others is another huge landscape for discovering latent or new passions and special activities that you both embrace.

And don't forget to take a risk or two. Perhaps neither of you dance. Try ballroom or Texas two-step or whatever. Maybe it will be an exercise or foreign language class. You figure it out. You can turn up or even turn around your marriage. With God's help you'll do it.

God's best to you!

Made in the USA
Columbia, SC
13 January 2020